Dear Parent:

Your child's love of reading starts here!

Every child learns to read in a different way and at his or her own speed. Some go back and forth between reading levels and read favourite books again and again. Others read through each level in order. You can help your young reader improve and become more confident by encouraging his or her interests and abilities. From books your child reads with you to the books he or she reads alone, there are I Can Read Books for every stage of reading:

SHARED READING
Basic language, word repetition, and whimsical illustrations, ideal for sharing with your emergent reader

BEGINNING READING
Short sentences, familiar words, and simple concepts for children eager to read on their own

READING WITH HELP
Engaging stories, longer sentences, and language play for developing readers

READING ALONE
Complex plots, challenging vocabulary, and high-interest topics for the independent reader

I Can Read Books have introduced children to the joy of reading since 1957. Featuring award-winning authors and illustrators and a fabulous cast of beloved characters, I Can Read Books set the standard for beginning readers.

A lifetime of discovery begins with the magical words **"I Can Read!"**

Visit www.icanread.ca for information
on enriching your child's reading experience.

I Can Read Book® is a trademark of HarperCollins Publishers

Roberta Bondar: Space Explorer
Text copyright © 2019 by HarperCollins Publishers Ltd.
Pictures © 2019 by Nick Craine.
All rights reserved. Published by Collins, an imprint of HarperCollins Publishers Ltd.

HarperCollins books may be purchased for educational, business, or sales promotional use through our Special Markets Department.

HarperCollins Publishers Ltd
Bay Adelaide Centre, East Tower
22 Adelaide Street West, 41st Floor
Toronto, Ontario, Canada
M5H 4E3

www.harpercollins.ca

Library and Archives Canada Cataloguing in Publication information is available upon request.

www.icanread.ca

ISBN 978-1-4434-5981-5

WZL 1 2 3 4 5 6 7 8 9 10

ROBERTA BONDAR:
SPACE EXPLORER

by Sarah Howden
pictures by Nick Craine

Collins

"I'm the luckiest person on
Earth," Roberta said to herself.
But she wasn't on Earth.
She was in space!

The day before, Roberta had boarded
the space shuttle *Discovery*.
It blasted off into the sky.

The ride had been rocky.

But the shuttle made it.

Now it was circling

around the Earth.

Roberta and the rest of the crew

would be in space for eight days.

There was no gravity in space.

Everything was weightless.

So Roberta was floating.

Roberta's coffee cup stayed
in mid-air when she let go of it.
"You can't do that back home,"
she said with a smile.

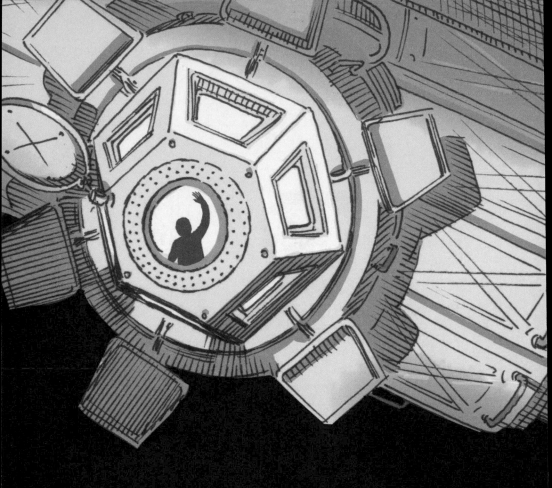

Just then something caught

Roberta's eye.

"Look!" she said to her

fellow astronauts.

"It's Earth!"

The planet filled the window.

The other astronauts came to see.

Roberta took some photos.
"I want people at home to see
this view," she said.
"It's incredible."

Roberta had wanted to be
an astronaut since she was a kid.
"I want to see the stars up close,"
she told her parents.

Roberta and her sister would pretend
to be space explorers.

"I'm on planet Zoot,"

Roberta would say.

"I will bring back space samples

to study."

Roberta had always loved science.
She loved it so much that her dad
made her a lab in the basement.

Roberta did science experiments.

She also built model rockets.

She was always dreaming of space.

Roberta grew up and became a doctor.

"Doctors save lives," she said.

"It's the most important

job there is."

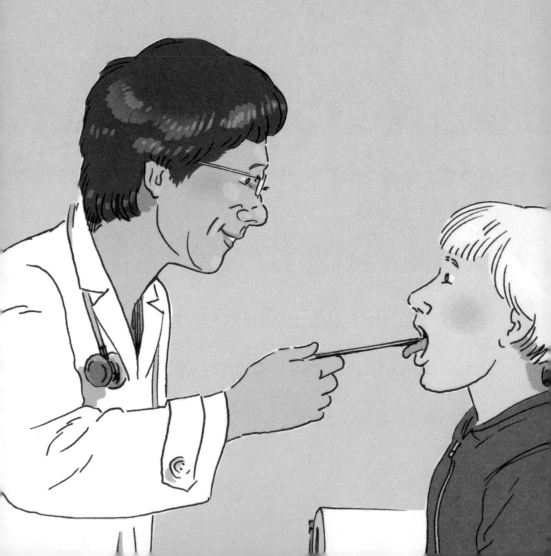

One day the Canadian Space Agency

put out a call for astronauts.

This was Roberta's chance.

"Only six people will be chosen,"
the agency said.

Thousands of people applied.

Roberta got in!

She trained for eight years.

She learned to parachute.

She learned how the shuttle worked.

Finally, launch day arrived.

The shuttle took off.

And Roberta became the first

Canadian woman in space.

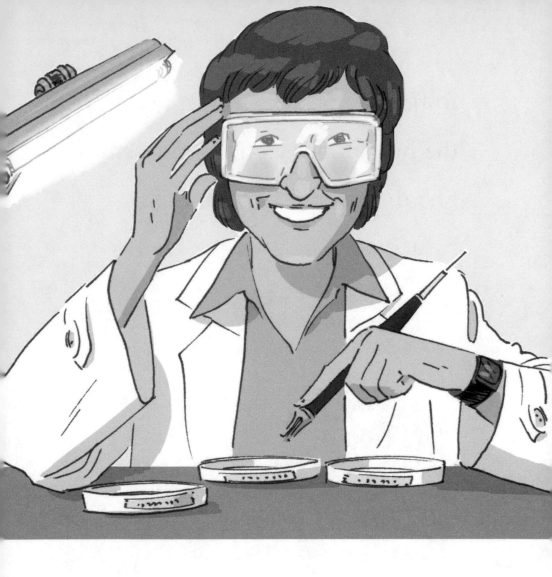

Life on the shuttle was busy.

Roberta did science experiments,

just like when she was little.

Roberta's job was to test how
the human body changed in space.
She discovered one thing
by accident.

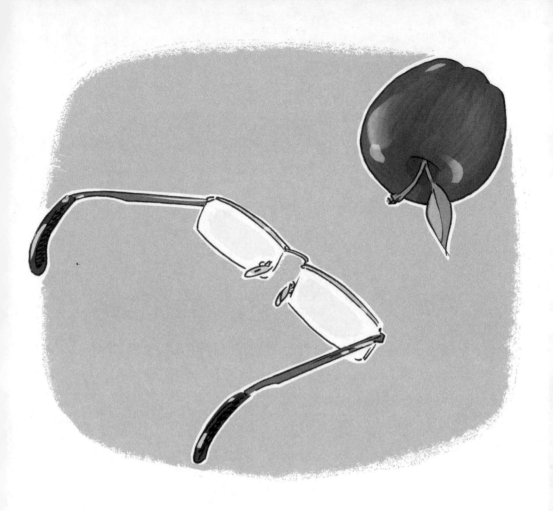

"I lost my glasses,"

Roberta told the crew.

"But I can still see."

"My eyes work better here,"

Roberta said,

"because there's no gravity!"

Roberta had brought a box of
Girl Guide cookies on the shuttle.
In a video to Earth, she juggled
them for all to see.

The cookies floated like magic.

Everyone watching was amazed.

Kids said, "Space looks fun!"

One week later Roberta was

back on Earth.

She had to get used to

gravity again.

Everything felt a lot heavier!

Soon Roberta was travelling to
schools to talk about her trip.
"There is still a lot to learn,"
she said.
"So we'll need more astronauts."

"Who wants to be an astronaut when they grow up?" Roberta asked.

Many kids raised their hands.

They wanted to be just like Roberta.

Do you want to be an astronaut?

Maybe one day you can go

to outer space too!